Animal Neighbors
Swallow

Stephen Savage

PowerKiDS press.

New York

Published in 2009 by The Rosen Publishing Group Inc.
29 East 21st Street, New York, NY 10010

First Edition

Commissioning Editor: Victoria Brooker
Produced by Nutshell Media
Editor: Polly Goodman
Designer: Tim Mayer
Illustrator: Jackie Harland

Library of Congress Cataloging-in-Publication Data

Savage, Stephen, 1965.
Swallow / Stephen Savage. — 1st ed.
p. cm. — (Animal neighbors)
ISBN 978-1-4358-4999-0 (library binding)
ISBN 978-1-4042-4576-1 (paperback)
ISBN 978-1-4042-4588-4 (6-pack)
1. Barn swallow—Juvenile literature. I. Title.
QL696.P247S26 2009
598.8'26—dc22
2008005457

Picture acknowledgements
FLPA 8 (Michael Jones), 9 (Hans Dieter Brandl), 12 (Roger Hosking), 15 (Ron Austing), 23 (H. D. Brandl), 28 top (Michael Jones), 28 left (H. D. Brandl); Natural Visions 16–17 (Jason Venus); naturepl.com Title page, 10, 28 right (Mike Wilkes); NHPA Cover, 7 (Stephen Dalton), 13 (Melvin Gray), 19, 21, 24 (Stephen Dalton), 26 (David Woodfall), 28 bottom (Melvin Gray); Oxford Scientific Films 6 (Frank Huber), 11 (John Gerlach/AA), 20 (Tony Tilford), 22 (Dennis Green/SAL), 25 (OSF), 27 (David Tipling); rspb-images.com 14 (Mark Hamblin).

Manufactured in China

Contents

Meet the Swallow   4

The Swallow Family   6

Birth and Growing Up   8

Habitat   14

Food and Hunting   18

Finding a Mate   22

Threats   24

Swallow Life Cycle   28

Swallow Clues   29

Glossary   30

Finding Out More and Web Sites   31

Index   32

Meet the Swallow

Swallows are graceful, acrobatic birds. There are over 50 species of swallow alive today. They can be found across Europe, Asia, North and South America, and northern and southern Africa.

This book looks at the barn swallow, the most widespread of all the swallow species.

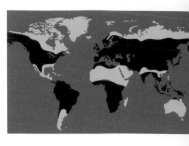

▲ The red shading on this map shows where barn swallows live.

Forked tail

The swallow's forked tail helps it change direction in the air. It can be turned or fanned out in the air to act as a brake when it is hunting flying insects.

Tail streamers

The barn swallow's tail streamers make it even more agile. Male barn swallows have extra-long tail streamers to attract females.

SWALLOW FACTS

The barn swallow's scientific name is *Hirundo rustica*, **which comes from the Latin words** *hirundo* **meaning "swallow," and** *rustica* **meaning "rural."**

Male swallows are about 5.5 in. (14 cm) long. Females are shorter, about 5 in. (12.5 cm). Swallows weigh 0.7 oz. (20 g).

Young swallows are called chicks.

▲ This shows the size of a swallow compared to an adult human hand.

4

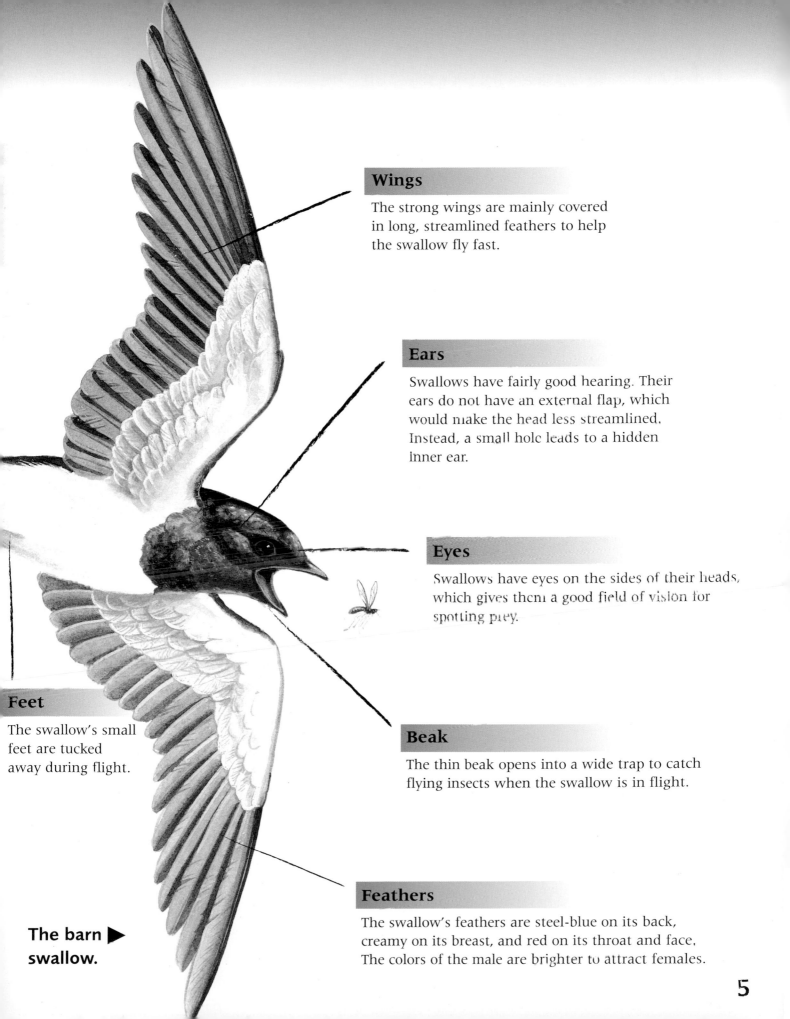

Wings

The strong wings are mainly covered in long, streamlined feathers to help the swallow fly fast.

Ears

Swallows have fairly good hearing. Their ears do not have an external flap, which would make the head less streamlined. Instead, a small hole leads to a hidden inner ear.

Eyes

Swallows have eyes on the sides of their heads, which gives them a good field of vision for spotting prey.

Beak

The thin beak opens into a wide trap to catch flying insects when the swallow is in flight.

Feet

The swallow's small feet are tucked away during flight.

Feathers

The swallow's feathers are steel-blue on its back, creamy on its breast, and red on its throat and face. The colors of the male are brighter to attract females.

The barn ▶ swallow.

5

The Swallow Family

There are 90 species in the swallow family, including swallows and martins. All members of this family are small birds, between 4 and 8 inches (10–20 cm) long. They all feed on flying insects and are strong fliers.

In the cold winter months, many species, such as the cliff swallow and the barn swallow, migrate hundreds of miles to warmer countries, where there is more food. Some species, such as the tree swallow, migrate shorter distances. This is because apart from insects, they also eat seeds and fruit.

▼ The tree swallow chooses a hole that is small enough to stop most predators getting at its nest.

▲ A house martin flies to its nest under the eaves of a house. House martins lack the swallow's long, forked tail.

Swallows make their nests in a variety of places. The cliff swallow makes a nest out of mud on cliff faces. The tree swallow nests in hollow trees or old woodpecker nest holes. The bank swallow and the sand martin make their nests in the sandbanks of rivers. Several species, such as the barn swallow and house martin, build their nests under the eaves of houses.

FEATHER FACTS

Feathers are the most distinctive characteristic of birds. They are made of keratin, which is similar to the substance that makes human hair and nails. Small feathers cover a bird's body and parts of the wing. They help keep the bird warm and dry. Long flight feathers on the bird's wings and tail are streamlined for fast and powerful flight.

Birth and Growing Up

It is April, and a female barn swallow prepares a nest, ready to lay her eggs. It might be in the rafters of a barn, under the eaves of a house, or sheltered beneath a bridge. Over the next few days, the female swallow lays up to six eggs, one at a time. As soon as they are laid, she sits on the eggs to incubate them while the chicks grow inside. Several times a day, the female carefully turns each egg using her beak, which helps the embryos to grow properly.

▼ In this nest, the first swallow egg has hatched and the parents have already removed the empty shell.

The swallow will incubate her eggs in this way for about 14 days until they are ready to hatch. During this time, she leaves the nest for only a few minutes each day, to stretch her wings and find food. Sometimes the male will help incubate the eggs or bring the female food.

After 14 days, the chicks peck their way out of the eggs. Swallow chicks hatch with their eyes closed and without feathers. Their first few days consist of sleeping and being fed by their parents. Between 8 and 10 days old, the chicks develop soft, downy feathers, which help keep them warm.

▲ Young swallow chicks huddle together to keep warm while the adults are away from the nest.

EGGS AND CHICKS

Swallow eggs are white and shiny, with brown or pale-gray speckles.

A group of eggs is called a clutch. A group of chicks is called a brood.

There can be between three and six eggs in a clutch, but the average number is four.

Early days

Feeding hungry chicks is a full-time job and both the male and female swallows collect insects for their young. The parent birds bring back several insects at a time, catching and compressing them into a ball before carrying them back to the nest in their throat.

Back at the nest, the hungry chicks compete for food. They call out with their beaks wide open, begging to be fed. Their bright orange gape is a signal to the parent birds, meaning, "Feed me, I'm hungry!" The chick with the loudest call and the brightest gape will always be fed first.

▲ When a parent returns with food, the chicks compete for attention with wide-open gapes.

STORM HAZARDS

A change in the weather can be disastrous for a swallow brood. An unexpected storm can threaten the chick's food supply, because flying insects remain in vegetation on the ground. The adults also remain grounded and cannot fly.

◄ After they have been fed, the chicks settle down in the nest to rest. Most of their energy at this time is used for growing.

When a chick has had enough to eat, it will rest. The parents continue their food trips until all the chicks are resting, making as many as 400 trips a day. They want to make sure that none of their chicks go without a meal.

11

First flights

In the nest, swallow chicks flap their wings regularly to strengthen their flight muscles. When they are about 20 days old, they are ready for their first flight. By now, they will have grown their adult feathers and are called fledglings. If its wings are strong enough, the fledgling's first flight will be successful. If not, it will crash to the ground.

For the next ten days or so, the fledglings stay in or near the nest as they practice other short flights. Their parents continue to feed them at first, but soon the fledglings will have to fend for themselves and leave the nest for the wide-open sky.

◀ **By the time the fledglings are 20 days old, the nest has become very crowded.**

Like their parents, young swallows very soon become excellent flyers, swooping and gliding for hours as they catch insects in the air. They follow their parents and other swallows to good feeding sites, where they perfect their hunting skills.

▼ Young fledglings who have just left the nest will roost together for some time, seeking safety in numbers.

Habitat

Barn swallows build their nests on structures built by people, such as barns, outbuildings, and bridges. In barns and other places with enough space, they sometimes form nesting colonies. A traditional barn can support up to eight swallows' nests.

Both the male and the female swallow build the nest. They build it using mud, straw, and sometimes horsehair. Many swallows return to the same nest site they used the previous year, to repair and reuse the old nest.

▼ This swallow is collecting mud to make its nest. A good source of mud may be visited by large numbers of swallows.

NEST BUILDING

To build or repair a nest, first the swallows search for a source of wet mud, often near water. They collect the mud in their beaks, make it into pellets, and carry it back to the nest site. The mud pellets are mixed with saliva and used to build a cup-shaped nest high above the ground. It takes about 1,000 trips to bring enough mud to make one nest.

Fledglings, and adult swallows who have raised their young and abandoned their nest, sleep together in roosts. These are usually in reed beds or wooded areas of trees and bushes. Sometimes more than 100,000 swallows roost together.

▲ The swallow's nest is built up of many layers of mud.

Migration

Every year barn swallows make a long journey called a migration. They spend the summer months in temperate regions such as Europe and North America, where there is plenty of insect food. During the winter months, when insects become scarce and their food supply runs out, swallows have to fly south to warmer regions.

▲ **This swallow is flying over the Sahara Desert in Morocco, on its route from Europe to South Africa.**

In the fall, swallows gather together in large flocks to make their long flight south. Older birds set off first, leaving the younger swallows to follow and learn the way.

Barn swallows can fly up to 186 miles (300 kilometers) in a single day. Their journey south can take up to three months. When the swallows return in the spring, their journey can take as little as two months, because they will be in a rush to mate.

PICKING A ROUTE

Swallows follow the same routes every year. These are mainly straight lines to their destination, which makes them the shortest possible routes. Swallows usually fly across seas at the narrowest point so they are over water for as short a time as possible, since few insects can be found above the sea. Many migrating birds have to stop flying regularly to feed. Swallows can travel farther than other birds without resting, because they catch insects in the air as they fly.

Swallows fly during the daylight, using the position of the Sun and other clues to help them find their way. The journey from Europe will take them across open seas, the Alps, and the Sahara Desert. A similar migration takes place in the Americas, from summer nesting sites in North America to winter sites in South America.

When they migrate over more difficult terrain, the swallows may form large roosts at night, seeking safety in numbers. They spend the winter months south of the Sahara Desert on the huge grasslands known as savannah, or on farmland or in towns.

▼ The arrows on this map show the main migration routes of barn swallows.

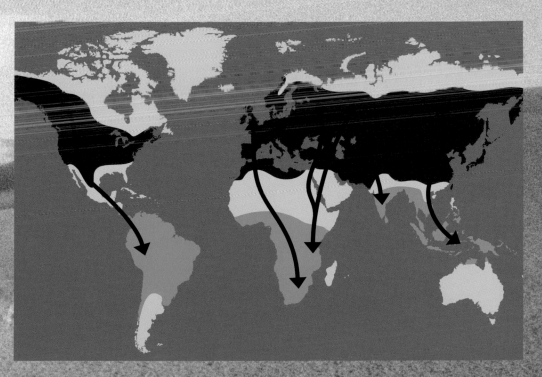

■ Summer breeding grounds

  Winter feeding grounds

Food and Hunting

Barn swallows are insectivores. They feed entirely on insects and other tiny creatures, most of which they catch in the sky. Their favorite prey is bluebottle flies and hoverflies.

When flying insects are scarce, such as during poor weather, swallows may be forced to catch prey on the ground, including beetles, grasshoppers, spiders, and the caterpillars of certain moths.

Swallow food chain

◄ Only fast-flying birds of prey, such as the kestrel, or sparrow hawk, are quick enough to catch the swallow. (The illustrations are not to scale.)

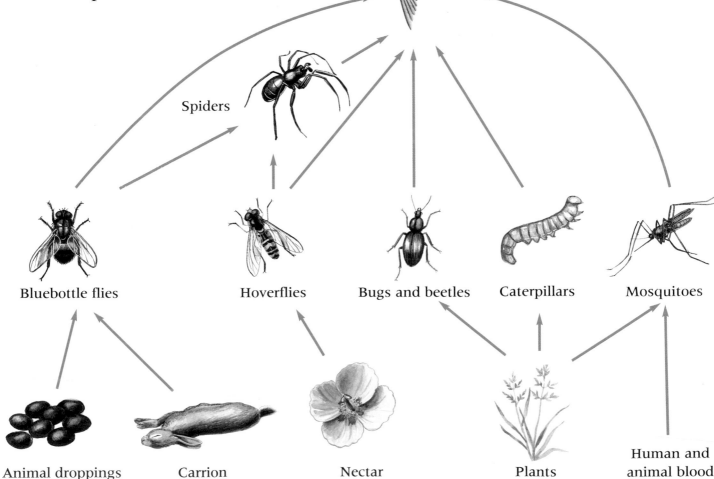

Birds of prey

Barn swallow

Spiders

Bluebottle flies

Hoverflies

Bugs and beetles

Caterpillars

Mosquitoes

Animal droppings

Carrion

Nectar

Plants

Human and animal blood

18

PREENING

Preening is an important daily activity that is essential for healthy feathers and successful flying. Birds use their beak to put their feathers back into place and spread a special oil over them, produced from a gland at the base of their tail. The oil keeps the feathers in good condition and makes them waterproof.

▲ A swallow leaves its nest inside a stable to start hunting for food outside.

The swallow is a fast, acrobatic flier. Even at great speeds, it can quickly change direction in pursuit of its prey. To help conserve energy, the swallow flies by making a series of rapid flaps with its wings, followed by a gentle glide. To catch the number of flying insects that it needs, swallows spend most of their waking hours in the air.

19

Hunting

Swallows find food anywhere that flying insects live in enough numbers. Most of their hunting is done near ground level, especially over open fields and farmland. However, on hot summer afternoons, flying insects are often found at higher altitudes because of rising warm air currents, so the swallow will fly higher to catch them.

▼ **During high-speed flight, the swallow tucks both legs up into its feathers and spreads its forked tail for balance.**

FAT RESERVES

In the fall, during the few weeks leading up to migration, the swallow must build up enough fat reserves to help it survive the long journey south. This means it has to eat a lot of insects. It has been estimated that a swallow searching for insects may fly over 600 miles (965 kilometers) in one day and eat as many as 6,000 insects.

▲ A swallow takes a drink from a river as it glides effortlessly above.

Ponds are another good place for catching insects as they flit about, just above the surface of the water. Swallows swoop down low over ponds to catch them. As it flies over a pond, the swallow can snatch a quick drink using its open beak to skim across the surface of the water.

Farmers and farm machinery often disturb insects. Swallows are attracted by this activity and the opportunity of easy hunting. They have also learned to follow grazing animals, whose movements through the grass also disturb insects.

Finding a Mate

Swallows are ready to breed by the time they are a year old, but not all will breed at first. Female swallows must find a fit, healthy male who will help her produce strong, healthy chicks. She can tell the health of a male from the brightness of his feathers and the length of his tail streamers.

▼ A male and female swallow. The female on the right can be recognized by its shorter tail feathers.

Swallows return to the area in which they hatched to breed. When a female has chosen her mate, she will lead him on a graceful courtship flight. At high speed, both birds fly around the nest site, swooping near the ground and then back up into the air. As they fly, both birds produce a constant twittering sound.

FOLKLORE

Some people believe it is a sign of good luck if a swallow chooses to nest on their house. Destroying a swallow's nest is thought to bring bad luck.

In ancient folklore, the swallow was thought to be a fire-bringer because of its red face markings.

Before people understood how and why birds migrated, some people thought that swallows either hibernated or flew to the moon.

When the female is satisfied with her choice, she lands on a roof or a tree and the male lands next to her. They may rub their heads together, hold each other's beaks, or preen each other's feathers before mating. Swallows usually pair for life, and the pair return to the same nest site each year.

▼ A pair of swallows mate while the female balances on a barbed wire fence.

Threats

▲ A kestrel, or sparrow hawk, uses its wings and tail feathers to slow down.

EARLY ALARM

In some parts of the world, barn swallows build their nests near those of ospreys. The swallows are protected from other birds of prey, which are driven away by the much larger ospreys. In return, the barn swallows alert the ospreys to the presence of these predators, which can be a danger to the osprey eggs or young in the nest.

Swallows can live for up to 7 years in the wild, but most only live to the age of 4. In Europe, the barn swallow has few natural predators due to its swift and acrobatic flight. Only a few birds of prey, such as the sparrow hawk and hobby, are capable of catching them in the air. It is the eggs and chicks in the nest that are most vulnerable, especially to birds of prey, crows, and magpies.

Pairs of swallows, sometimes with the help of their neighbors, defend the area around their nest and drive off intruders. They will chase away any swallows that try to take over their nesting site, and defend it against predators, such as birds of prey and domestic cats. Swallows living in a colony will mob an intruder by dive-bombing it.

Chicks are also threatened by parasites living in the nest, which bite them and suck their blood. Some parasites attach themselves to the chicks' eyes or enter their nostrils. A large number of parasites can kill swallow chicks, especially in the second brood, when there are more parasites in the nest.

▼ Under a microscope, you can can see the claws of a swallow parasite. The parasite holds onto chicks with these claws, which makes it difficult to shake off.

Habitat loss

As old barns are replaced with newer structures, swallows are losing one of their habitats. They are also threatened by the wide use of pesticides on farms, which wipe out the swallows' insect prey. This can have a dramatic effect on nesting swallows. The parent birds are forced to fly farther from the nest to collect insects for their young. If they cannot find enough food, their young can starve.

ARTIFICIAL NESTS

It is possible for people to help swallows in their area by buying and putting up artificial nests under the eaves of their house. Artificial nests can be attached to any surface, whereas natural mud nests will only stick to rough surfaces. This means that artificial nests can exist in many more places than natural nests.

▼ When pesticides are sprayed on crops, they kill the swallow's insect food.

▲ A barn swallow, blown off course and exhausted.

Migration hazards

Migration can be a hazardous time. Apart from the dangers of birds of prey, swallows risk being blown off course during storms. As they cross the sea, they can be forced to take shelter on ships or lighthouses. As they fly over mountain ranges, they often have to shelter in isolated buildings. Swallows crossing the Sahara Desert fly lower than most other migratory birds, which means they can get caught in sandstorms and die from exhaustion.

Swallow Life Cycle

1 Swallow eggs hatch after an incubation of 14–16 days. The chicks are born with their eyes closed and without feathers.

2 By 8–10 days old, the chicks are covered in downy feathers and their eyes are open.

3 At about 20 days old, the chicks are fully fledged and able to fly. The fledglings leave the nest when they are about 30 days old.

4 In the fall, the young swallows gather together for their long migration south.

5 In the spring, the swallows arrive in the north, ready to breed.

Swallow Clues

Look for the following clues to help you find signs of a swallow:

Nest
The round, bowl-shaped nest can be seen under the eaves of houses, or in barns and other outbuildings.

Feeding young
Because swallows build their nests so close to human homes, you can easily see them coming and going as they feed their young.

Nest making
Swallows can be seen gathering mud from the edges of ponds in the spring. Sometimes many pairs of swallow will collect nest material from the same place.

Gathering for migration
A good time to see swallows is when they gather in large flocks, ready for their migration.

Call
Swallows make a cheerful "vit vit" call when flying. They make a "pss-st…pss-st" call at the sight of a bird of prey, such as a kestrel or hobby.

Droppings
The swallow's droppings are runny and white, just like any other bird. Lots of droppings on the ground under the eaves of a house or barn may be a sign there is a swallow's nest above.

Silhouette
The swallow's distinctive silhouette makes it distinguishable from similar-sized birds, such as the swift and the house martin.

Barn swallow

House martin

Swift

The illustrations are not to scale.

Glossary

bird of prey A bird that hunts animals for food.

brood A group of chicks born at the same time.

carrion The body of a dead animal that is found and eaten by another animal.

clutch A number of eggs laid at the same time by one female.

colony A group of the same type of animals that live together.

downy Soft and fluffy.

embryos The early stages of development of a bird inside its egg before hatching, or any unborn animal.

field of vision The view an animal has from both eyes without moving its head.

fledgling The stage in a young bird's development when it has just learned to fly.

flock A group of birds.

gape The opening of a young bird's mouth to show the bright color inside, giving a signal that it wants to be fed.

habitat The area where an animal or plant naturally lives.

incubate To hatch eggs by sitting on them to keep them warm.

insectivore An animal that eats mainly insects.

migrate To travel between different habitats or countries in particular seasons.

osprey A large fish-eating bird of prey.

parasite An animal or a plant, such as a flea, that lives on another living thing without giving any benefit in return.

predator An animal that kills and eats other animals.

prey Animals that are killed and eaten by predators.

roost A place where birds gather to rest or sleep, or the action of birds when they rest or sleep.

streamlined Shaped to help fly through the air with little effort.

temperate A type of climate that is neither very hot nor very cold.

Finding Out More

Other books to read

Animal Babies: Birds by Rod Theodorou
(Heinemann, 2007)

Attracting and Feeding Backyard Birds by Carol
Frischmann (TFH Publications, 2007)

Classifying Living Things: Classifying Birds by
Andrew Solway (Heinemann, 2003)

From Egg to Adult: The Life Cycle of Birds by Mike
Unwin (Heinemann, 2003)

*Illustrated Encyclopedia of Animals in Nature and
Myth* by Fran Pickering (Chrysalis, 2003)

Life Cycles: Ducks and Other Birds by Sally Morgan
(Chrysalis, 2001)

Living Nature: Birds by Angela Royston
(Chrysalis, 2004)

What's the Difference?: Birds by Stephen Savage
(Raintree, 2002)

Web Sites

Due to the changing nature of Internet links,
PowerKids Press has developed an online list of
Web Sites related to the subject of this book. This
site is updated regularly. Please use this link to
access this list:
www.powerkidslinks.com/ani/swallow

Index

Page numbers in **bold** refer to a photograph or illustration.

beak **5**, 10, 19

call 10, 22, 29

chicks 4, **7**, **8**, **9**, **10**, **11**, 22, 24, 25, **28**

colonies 14, 25

distribution **4**

drinking **21**

droppings 29

eggs **8**, 9, 13, 24, **28**

embryos 8

feathers **5**, 7, 9, 19, **28**

feet **5**

females 4, 5, 8, 9, 14, **22**, **23**

fledglings **12**, **13**, 15, **28**

flight **5**, **7**, 12, 13, **16**, 17, **19**, **20**, 22, 28

folklore 23

food 6, 9, **10**, 11, 12, 13, 16, 18–21, 26

habitats 14, 15, 17, 26

hatching **8**, 9

houses **7**, 8, 26, 29

hunting 13, **20–21**

incubate 8, 9, 28

insects 4, **5**, 6, 10, 11, 13, 16, **18**, 19, 20, 21, 26

lifespan 24

males 4, 5, 9, 10, 14, **22**, **23**

mating **22–23**, **28**

migration 6, **16–17**, 21, 23, 27, 28, 29

nests 6, **7**, **8**, **9**, **12**, 14, **15**, 23, 24, 25, 26, **29**

parasites **25**

predators **18**, **24**, 25, 27, 29

preening 19

prey **5**, **18**, 19, 26

roosts **13**, 15, 17

seasons 16, 20

size **4**

swallow species 4, **6–7**

  cliff swallow 6, 7

  house martin **7**, **29**

  sand martin 7

  tree swallow **6**, 7

tail **4**, **7**, **20**

weather 11, 18

wings **5**, 12